FILOLI, Woodside, California. Camellia.

(Page 1) NAUMKEAG, Stockbridge, Massachusetts. Garden bench detail.

Published by Thomasson-Grant, Inc.: Frank L. Thomasson III and John F. Grant, Directors;
C. Douglas Elliott, Vice President, Product Development; Carolyn M. Clark, Creative Director;
Mary Alice Parsons, Art Director; Hoke Perkins, Senior Editor.

Designed by Leonard G. Phillips
Edited by Hoke Perkins and Owen Andrews

Concept development and research by Judith Helm Robinson, Elizabeth Jo Lampl,
and Julianne Mueller, Robinson & Associates, Washington, D.C.

Color separations by Pioneer Graphic through CGI (Malaysia) Sdn. Bhd.
Printed and bound in Singapore by Eurasia Press (Offset), Pte. Ltd.

96   95   94   93   92   91   90   89   5   4   3   2   1

Any inquiries should be directed to Thomasson-Grant, Inc.,
One Morton Drive, Suite 500, Charlottesville, Virginia 22901, telephone (804) 977-1780.

Library of Congress Cataloging-in-Publication Data
McGuire, Diane Kostial.
Gardens of America.
1. Gardens — United States — History. 2. Gardens —
United States — Design — History. 3. Gardening — United
States — History. 4. Gardens — United States — Pictorial
works. I. Title.
SB451.3.M34   1989   712'.0973   89-50584
ISBN 0-934738-53-X

GARDENS *of* AMERICA
THREE CENTURIES OF DESIGN

TEXT BY DIANE KOSTIAL MCGUIRE

THOMASSON-GRANT
CHARLOTTESVILLE, VIRGINIA

CONTENTS

SONNENBERG, Canandaigua, New York. Italian Garden.

I LIVE ON THE FOG-BOUND COAST OF RHODE ISLAND, WHERE HOUSES and gardens are intimately related to the sea, and farms reflect the long years of labor that brought them into being. The beauty of this land influences my work as a landscape architect, and its history inspires me to help restore other American places.

The spirit of preservation has swept America only recently. Earlier in this century, the historic buildings and green spaces that gave many older communities their character were neglected. Thousands of architectural treasures were demolished in the postwar economic boom. In the late 1960s and early 1970s, the emergence of a grassroots conservation movement and widespread interest in the upcoming Bicentennial changed this state of affairs. Towns all across the country raised funds to restore courthouses, churches, and historic neighborhoods.

Before long, preservationists broadened their efforts to include gardens. Spurred by the energy of the women's garden clubs, Americans searched old diaries, travelers' accounts, and garden plans for historically authentic plant varieties and landscape designs. Gardeners at historic sites began to plant herb beds based on what colonists might have grown and to cultivate the exotics and hybrids that made 19th-century flower beds so delightful. This interest in older plants has led directly to today's passion for creating herbaceous borders in suburban gardens and for using Victorian-style displays of vividly-colored flowers to adorn apartments.

The gardens explored in this book have been chosen for their horticultural beauty and historically accurate design. Originally private domestic gardens, most are now open to the public. Some display distinctly American contributions to garden design; others reveal the genius Americans have always had for adapting European styles to New World cultures and climates. Whether they are world-famous shrines like Mount Vernon or recently restored jewels like Celia Thaxter's Garden, these places honor the talent of America's gardeners and landscape architects and the ingenuity of its preservationists.

—*Diane Kostial McGuire*

MONTICELLO, Charlottesville, Virginia. Thomas Jefferson changed his gardens and grounds continually as his interests evolved. Today, they vary from year to year, reflecting historians' most recent discoveries.

7

EARLY GARDENS
OF USEFUL PLANTS

On any wilderness homestead, a thriving garden is a symbol of survival, evidence that a desperate enterprise has become a domestic haven. After clearing the land for their fields and houses, American colonists built communities that contrasted vividly with the surrounding forest. They organized their settlements into neat geometric spaces; fields and woodlots ringed the towns, and orchards and kitchen gardens bracketed the houses.

The first New England colonists knew they would have to provide not only grains, vegetables, and fruits, but the plants they used for medicines and other household needs. Once established, they also had to provision later settlers. Examples of these gardens of useful plants are rare because their restoration calls for painstaking research. One of the most authentic colonial gardens forms a courtyard in front of the 17th-century John Whipple House in Ipswich, Massachusetts. American landscape historian Ann Leighton re-created the garden based on letters, wills, and travelers' accounts of the time.

A wooden fence with a narrow gate separates the garden from the adjoining common. Within the fence are six raised beds, each contained by boards secured with wooden pegs. Raising the beds provided good drainage, and because the soil in them thawed quickly, they could be planted early in spring. The beds are filled with nearly 100 kinds of vegetables and herbs, so densely planted that they resemble bouquets, fragrant and varied in color and texture.

John Josselyn's *New-Englands Rarities Discovered*, published in London in 1672, is the most useful reference for the identification of plants grown by the colonists. His book was based on two sojourns in New England in the 1630s and 1660s. Unlike many early garden writers, Josselyn wrote directly from his own observations, and his book has been used in the restoration of several New England gardens.

In the early days, colonists relied on plants grown from seeds they brought with them. Gradually, they began to experiment with vegetables introduced to them by the

WHIPPLE HOUSE, Ipswich, Massachusetts. Early New England settlers cultivated an abundance of vegetables and herbs to make their households self-sufficient. Ferns were among the plants they used as medicine. One 17th-century botanist reported that "tops and nudicaments of sweet fern boiled in water and milk helpeth all manner of fluxes, being boiled in water it makes an excellent liquor for Inck."

Indians, most notably corn. They also learned to relish another staple of the native diet, the "earth-nut," probably a form of flowering wild bean. Any plant had to be hardy and productive to find a place in colonial gardens. Many European plants took so well to the climate that they spread into meadows and along roadsides; yarrow, tansy, feverfew, and butterfly weed, originally nurtured for their medicinal values, are now a familiar part of the New England countryside.

In colonial times, women supervised households and gardens while men tilled the fields and took care of the livestock and orchards. Hence, the garden of useful plants was placed close to the house, only a few paces from the kitchen and still-room, where the housewife distilled various concoctions for her family. Her garden provided ingredients for syrups and pills devised to remedy a variety of complaints. Plants also helped stanch and salve wounds, and the more fragrant ones were used to make insecticides and deodorants. Some plants were reputed to relieve the pain of labor, and others helped prepare bodies for burial.

Seventeenth-century English botanist John Parkinson described many specific uses for these plants. Dried lavender flowers, he wrote, "comfort and dry up the moisture of a cold braine." Sorrel used in a sauce cools "hot livers and stomackes." And Parkinson reported of dill that some people "eat the seed to stay the Hickocke."

The orchard was also laid out close to the house. At first, colonists grew familiar European apples, pears, peaches, and plums, but soon adapted varieties for the harsher American climate. The Whipple House pear orchard follows the quincunx pattern: four trees arranged in a square with a fifth in the center. Other elaborate orchards in the colonies displayed cordoned and espaliered fruit trees, but most, regardless of their size, were much simpler.

New England's domestic orchards, so diligently established in the 1700s, remained a part of the landscape until well into this century, when the advent of long-distance fruit shipping made them obsolete. The garden of useful plants vanished earlier, as medicine, once the housewife's domain, became a profession dominated by scientific methods and by men.

SHERBURNE HOUSE, Strawberry Banke, Portsmouth, New Hampshire. Old stake holes helped archeologists locate the raised beds behind the Sherburne House, and pollen remains helped identify the original plants.

(Facing) WHIPPLE HOUSE. Paling fences kept stray livestock out of herb and vegetable gardens.

WHIPPLE HOUSE. White, bell-shaped lily of the valley blossoms (above) stand out in a bed of herbs. Lily of the valley was ingested for a variety of complaints from gout to inflammation of the eyes to faulty memory. Captain John Whipple's 1683 inventory of his house noted several medicines made from plants in the garden, including ''five bottles of syrup of clove gilly flowers.''

WHIPPLE HOUSE. *Two old rose varieties, Seven Sisters and Harrison's Yellow (above), cover an 18th-century-style trellis in a garden to the side of the house. Along with pansies and other modest flowers, roses were grown for decoration. They were also distilled into fragrant waters and pain-killing cordials. Simple floral displays and straight, intersecting paths (facing) lent a functional grace to these early gardens.*

BARTRAM'S GARDEN

John Bartram, one of the colonies' first botanists, was described by a friend as a "down right plain country man." Born into a Pennsylvania farming family, he was inspired to teach himself botany by one of the commonest of flowers, the daisy. But this simple man, who devoted his life to collecting, cultivating, and disseminating plants, became a major·figure in 18th-century horticulture. With Benjamin Franklin, he was one of the founders of the American Philosophical Society, the colonies' first professional scientific organization. More important, many of America's historic gardens were created with plants he discovered or provided.

Forced as a boy to work on his family's farm after only four years of school, Bartram later asked a local schoolmaster to help him learn Latin so that he could read scientific texts by men such as the Swedish botanist Carolus Linnaeus. In turn, Linnaeus, the father of systematic plant taxonomy, would one day have reason to respect Bartram. When Linnaeus's assistant Peter Kalm visited America in the late 1740s, he made a point of traveling to Bartram's farm. Kalm later wrote:

> He has in several and successive years made frequent excursions into different distant parts of North America with an intention of gathering all sorts of plants which are scarce and little-known....I have often been at a loss to think of the sources whence he obtained so many things which came to his knowledge. I, also, owe him much, for he possessed that great quality of communicating everything he knew.

Linnaeus received rare new plants from Bartram's travels, excursions that took the Philadelphian from Florida to Lake Ontario. Among the plants Bartram gathered in the Carolina swamps was the Venus's-flytrap, which he called the "Tipitiwitchet." London merchant Peter Collinson, one of the men responsible for shipping Bartram's plants, sent the flytrap to Linnaeus, predicting that he would be "in raptures at the sight of it."

Collinson, Bartram's friend and fellow Quaker, distributed the collector's North American plants and seeds to English landowners for 30 years. Bartram received goods in return, most notably English wildflower seeds from Philip Miller's renowned Chelsea Physick Garden. He cultivated these and many other European plants and distributed them to

BARTRAM'S GARDEN, Philadelphia, Pennsylvania. John Bartram built his house from stone he quarried on his own. The six-acre botanical garden that stretched from the house down to the Schuylkill River was stocked with plants, shrubs, and trees he collected on his travels in North America, including the sycamore (facing) towering over the side lawn. Behind the house, Bartram planted a display garden he called his Common Garden (above) with over 50 kinds of flowers and herbs.

American collectors. Bartram's and Collinson's letters tell much about the hazards of 18th-century botanical science, from the difficulties of shipping delicate plants across the stormy Atlantic to the dangers of collecting samples in the wilderness. Bartram once faced down an Indian who blocked his path, snatched up his hat, and chewed it as a warning.

Through Bartram, Collinson obtained trees, shrubs, bulbs, and seeds for his patrons, among them the Prince of Wales and the Dukes of Richmond, Norfolk, and Bedford. Many English gardens established or redesigned in the early 18th century incorporated North American plants. Especially enchanting is the wilderness at Wales's Powis Castle in the fall. There, set among a large grove of English oaks, grow trees familiar to Americans: pale silver maples, deep yellow tulip poplars, and glistening red sourwoods.

One English gardener of the time chided his countrymen for a sort of hysteria that led them to think any North American plant was intrinsically valuable. The trade in plants supported several nurseries besides Bartram's, including one founded by Robert Prince on Long Island in 1737. Collinson and his correspondents, however, never doubted the utility of Bartram's work; one of Collinson's letters lists over 100 species shipped to England, "the largest collection that had ever before been imported into this Kingdom." The English court considered North American plants important enough that in 1765 Bartram was appointed Royal Botanist to King George III, receiving £50 a year for his services.

Americans paid homage to Bartram's work, as well; the Constitutional Convention recessed on July 14, 1787 to see the collection, managed by his sons after his death in 1777. George Washington also made a personal visit to Bartram's Nurseries that summer. He ordered many trees and shrubs for Mount Vernon, but noted that Bartram's farm was neither large nor "laid off with much taste." Bartram's garden was not laid out in an overarching design, for his aim was scientific rather than aesthetic, and his talent as a collector helped make possible the gardens of innovative landscape designers like Washington.

BARTRAM'S GARDEN. Bartram disseminated many trees, including yellowwood (above) and black maple (facing). The garden's rarest tree is the Franklinia, which Bartram discovered and named for his friend Benjamin Franklin; none have been seen in the wild since shortly after Bartram's son William collected seeds in Georgia in 1775.

BARTRAM'S GARDEN. Bartram's farm included a stableyard (facing), kitchen garden for his wife and nine children, and 100 acres of woodlands and fields. On this surrounding land Bartram pioneered the use of natural cultivating habitats; he nurtured many plants from his collection in environmental niches that suited their specific needs. A cross-vine (above) had climbed some 20 feet up the wall of the house by 1763, and he exported its seeds to England.

COLONIAL RIVER PLANTATIONS

From the Chesapeake Bay to Georgia's Sea Islands, the estuaries and rivers that divide the gentle slopes of the Atlantic coastal plain served as the highways of the colonial South. The first generations of settlers followed watercourses inland, choosing high ground near coves, inlets, and creeks for towns and plantation houses. Once farming was underway, cash crops were shipped from each planter's dock to the few large towns—Savannah, Charleston, Baltimore—or directly to England.

In this waterborne economy, where roads remained primitive well into the 19th century, planters faced their houses' main entrances toward the water. Early dwellings were simple, but as agricultural profits mounted toward the end of the 17th century, grand places arose, most notably along the James River in Virginia and the Ashley River in South Carolina. Naturally, planters who included elaborate gardens in their plans laid them out toward the river, where they could immediately impress the arriving traveler. Thus the falls garden appeared, characterized by landscaped terraces and walks that elegantly linked land and water.

One of the most impressive falls gardens ever constructed survives at Middleton Place on the Ashley River. Here, a prosperous rice planter named Henry Middleton kept 100 slaves laboring for 10 years to build a 110-acre complex of formal gardens, terraces, and artificial lakes.

Middleton, who later served as second president of the First Continental Congress, began the gardens in 1741. The famous terraces completely shape the point of land where the house sits, descending in five levels to two wing-shaped pools known as the Butterfly Lakes. Narrow banks divide them from two larger ponds, beyond which the Ashley flows. From the house, these bodies of still water create a controlled prospect toward the river; from the river, the terraces communicate the power and wealth of the Middleton family.

MIDDLETON PLACE, Charleston, South Carolina. Ancient live oaks shade the perimeters of the great lawns at Middleton Place. The oldest, called the Middleton Oak, has a limb spread of 145 feet. Home to a family that included a president of the First Continental Congress, a signer of the Declaration of Independence, and a governor of South Carolina and minister to Russia, the house at Middleton Place is only one wing of the original mansion, which was destroyed over the years by fire, war, and earthquake.

The grandeur and formality of Middleton Place have no parallel among other American plantations of the time; Henry Middleton looked to England and France for his plan, which shows the influence of André Le Nôtre, the great 17th-century French landscape designer. Le Nôtre's works included the gardens at Versailles, Fontainebleau, and Vaux-le-Vicomte, and his ideas were widely copied in late 17th- and early 18th-century Europe. Perhaps Middleton invited an English or French imitator of Le Nôtre to South Carolina to oversee his project, or worked from plans of estates he visited on European travels.

At Middleton Place, the influence of Le Nôtre is evident not only in the lakes and terraces, but in the 650-foot-long reflecting pool and the formal parterres—geometrically patterned hedges and flower beds. These strictly proportioned elements are aligned within the form of a right triangle. As in Le Nôtre's designs, secluded spots provide a contrast to the plan's expansive prospects. Even today, when only one wing of the house stands, a sense of civilized order reigns amid Middleton Place's ancient trees and wide lawns.

Along the James River between Richmond and Williamsburg, William Byrd II and several other Virginia tobacco planters also terraced the land between their Georgian mansions and the water. But their falls gardens were much simpler than those at Middleton Place, and around their mansions flower beds and plantings followed old Tudor English patterns. Large, square beds of vegetables grew close to the house; nearby, beds of flowering plants enclosed by walls or arbors featured heraldic and Masonic insignias or medieval knot patterns, rather than French-inspired geometric motifs.

Colonial garden design differed sharply from European models in one respect: the South's sweltering summers compelled planters to use trees primarily for shade, not decoration. Discussing the issue in a letter to a friend, Thomas Jefferson observed of English gardeners that

their sunless climate has permitted them to adopt what is certainly a beauty of the very first order in landscape. Their canvas is of open ground, variegated with clumps of trees distributed with taste. They need not more of wood than will serve to embrace a lawn or a glade. But under our beaming, constant and almost vertical sun of Virginia, shade is our Elysium. In the absence of this no beauty of the eye can be enjoyed.

MIDDLETON PLACE. One of only two statues known to have survived the ransacking of the plantation during the Civil War, a marble wood nymph watches over a riverside flower garden.

Choosing shade trees, planters naturally turned to the wilderness around them, full of species unknown in the Old World. The most widely admired American tree was the southern magnolia, then called the Laurel Tree of Carolina. Its evergreen leaves provided shade year-round, and its glistening, majestic presence lent dignity to any landscape. Another magnolia, the cucumber tree, was one of the most popular species in John Bartram's nursery. For areas near the house, landowners prized the tulip poplar, a magnificent tree that grows rapidly and puts out green and orange blossoms in the spring.

Colonists also favored elm, sweet gum, live oak, and catalpa. Their interest in New World trees coincided with the awakening of botanical science in Europe, as Linnaeus's new ways of classifying and analyzing plants stimulated collectors to search worldwide for rare and unusual species. Some of the trees and shrubs which planters brought into their plantation gardens were soon being cultivated on European estates as well. For example, seeds of the wild catalpa and many other trees were collected in the Piedmont and sent to English landowners and horti-culturalists by Mark Catesby, the English naturalist who dedicated his life to the first illustrated work on North American plants and animals. Catesby was a friend and guest of William Byrd II; the planter noted in his diary that his visitor "directed how I should mend my garden and put it into better fashion than it is at present." In later years, Catesby published a guide to the cultivation of American tree species in England.

Catesby's guide served not only botanists, but proponents of England's newly fashionable natural school of landscaping, who incorporated wild-seeming groves in rolling, unsymmetrical sequences of meadows and foliage. Thus, while American landowners were imitating French formalism, English aristocrats were changing the look of their estates with imported American trees.

MIDDLETON PLACE. The French explorer and botanist, André Michaux, a friend of the Middleton family, introduced the camellia to South Carolina. One camellia from Michaux's original planting has bloomed in the garden at Middleton Place since 1786.

MIDDLETON PLACE. Middleton is the quin-
tessential example of an 18th-century American
formal estate. While naturalistic elements were
added in the 19th century, including the azaleas
planted along the riverbank (facing), most of
the garden has kept its original character, with
classical statues and urns anchoring open
greenswards (above).

MIDDLETON PLACE. Middleton's peacocks (above) echo the radial forms of its famous "falls," or earthwork terraces (facing). One hundred slaves spent 10 years constructing Middleton's formal gardens, Butterfly Lakes, and terraces.

MIDDLETON PLACE. *Resurrection ferns (above), native to the Low Country, shrivel up and look lifeless in drought. When rain comes, the fronds unfurl. The symmetrical pattern of the Sundial Garden (facing) reveals the unknown designer's reliance upon French design, especially Le Nôtre's gardens at Versailles. Like many 18th-century gardens, Middleton follows a strict geometry, based on an isosceles right triangle with the sundial near the center of its hypotenuse.*

(Facing) BRANDON, Prince George County, Virginia. The wide, grassy path leading from the James River to the house at Brandon is one of the world's most beautiful garden walks. Its borders contain masses of the common blue iris frequently mentioned by 18th-century Virginia gardeners like Lady Skipwith and Thomas Jefferson.

(Above) WESTOVER, Charles City, Virginia. A wrought-iron fence defines the forecourt of William Byrd's James River plantation. A beehive, a pine-apple, and other carved stone finials representing garden objects cap each sectional pier—rare decorations in American gardens of the early 18th century.

ORNAMENTAL FARMS AND PLEASURE GROUNDS

Renaissance aristocrats in Florence and Rome built their country villas on hillsides which commanded far-reaching views over fields and vineyards. Over time, their preference for a prospect acquired the status of a grand architectural idea, and passed from Italy to England, and ultimately, the New World, where it was put to characteristically practical use by two of America's most original and prominent gardeners, George Washington and Thomas Jefferson.

When Washington inherited Mount Vernon, he recognized the beauty of the house's site on a bluff beside the Potomac River and built a spacious porch to make the most of it. He then planned his landscape to shape the views: trees framed a prospect down the Potomac from the new porch, and his west windows looked out to a wide lawn. For his house, Washington's fellow Virginian Thomas Jefferson chose a mountaintop overlooking the Blue Ridge to the west and the coastal plain to the east. In homage to Italian inspiration, Washington called his porch a "piazza," and Jefferson named his home Monticello, or "little mountain."

While they took some ideas directly from classical and Renaissance models, both men also adapted ideas from the English natural school, which completely dominated landscaping in Britain by the mid-18th century. Books like Batty Langley's *New Principles of Gardening* and Thomas Whately's *Observations of Modern Gardening* guided, but did not determine the founding fathers' designs. In general, English naturalism rejected French geometric formalism and called for the combination of garden and countryside into a pastoral, picturesque landscape. On their ornamental farms, Washington and Jefferson mixed formal and informal elements, keeping the principle of utility constantly in sight.

Washington's plan for Mount Vernon is a masterpiece of landscape art, a flawless blend of beauty and function. His concept was ambitious; he landscaped a full 500 acres of his 8,000-acre estate. Washington placed his outbuildings and gardens on the house's entrance side, away from his grand river vistas, but gracefully linked to the house. From the

MOUNT VERNON, Mount Vernon, Virginia. Upon taking possession of his property, George Washington joined the outbuildings to the main house with colonnades and embellished the entrance courtyard with a sundial at the center of the circular lawn, creating a practical and harmonious design.

air, the gardens resemble arched windows, with the tips at the furthest point from the house. As a visitor approaches the house on the bell-shaped, tree-lined drive, the flower garden lies to the left, and the vegetable garden to the right, enclosed by matching brick walls topped with elegantly curved picket fences. Along these walls, four "pepper-pot" out-buildings—two at the corners nearest the house and two at the points of the arches—enhance the geometrical unity of house and garden.

On paper, Washington's plan for Mount Vernon is symmetrical, but on the ground, the juxtaposition of open meadows and groves around the house seems informal. The groves were Washington's special concern; his records and correspondence show his constant interest in the placement and nurture of his trees. He brought native saplings from the woods and created a "wilderness" by planting them in thick stands along the carriage drive.

The result was a bold and innovative approach to the house. In most estates of the period, the entrance drive stood clearly in the open, but Mount Vernon's drive curves through trees, providing passing views of the wide lawn, called the bowling green, that stretches out before the house. In Washington's plan for Mount Vernon, the strange and wild wood becomes the familiar grove—a fitting setting for the house of a man who spent his youth as a surveyor and soldier in the American wilderness.

Washington designed the grounds at Mount Vernon all at once, and made sure his gardeners closely followed his plans. In contrast, many of Jefferson's plans for garden projects were never realized. Unlike Washington, he traveled widely in Europe, making a point of visiting beautifully designed and landscaped estates. He was much more impressed than Washington by fanciful European landscapes; after his 1786 trip to England with John Adams, he lamented that America lacked craftsmen able to execute such sophisticated garden designs. But he noted that at Blenheim, one of England's grandest estates, "art appears too much." Always guided by this sense of restraint, Jefferson's plans

MOUNT VERNON. Redbud and dogwood trees blossom in early spring next to the "pepper pot" schoolhouse. Originally a seedhouse, the school-house is tucked into the corner at the far end of the flower garden; a matching toolhouse occupies the same place in the kitchen garden.

for Monticello changed as his knowledge grew, and the gardens which exist represent only a fraction of his horticultural ideas.

Like Washington, Jefferson was a lifelong collector of rare and unusual plants. He ordered seeds of North American plants from nurseries like Bartram's and cultivated native Virginia trees and shrubs, making a place in his groves and beds for several species of holly, rhododendron, and magnolia. A ceaseless experimenter, he tested varieties of grapes, hoping to create American wines, and planted mulberry trees and stocked them with silkworms. He also acquired exotic trees, including acacia, lime, sour orange, and fig.

Jefferson used a windowed porch of his house, the South Piazza, as a greenhouse for some of his tender plants. But their existence was precarious: his "frequent and long absences" left them unattended. Washington was more successful, and erected a fine orangery for his exotics in 1785. Unlike present day greenhouses, it had only one glazed wall. He used the orangery to protect the less hardy plants (including the forerunner of the grapefruit) that friends and admirers sent him from all over the world.

Jefferson's love for his collection led him to create the most striking element of his landscape design, the western garden walk, a serpentine path that winds in a loose oval along beds and borders of flowers as fascinating as they are beautiful. Reaching the crest of the broad hill, the path offers views of mountains, fields, valleys, and then, as it curves back toward the house, centers attention on Jefferson's simple Palladian masterpiece.

Early in the 18th century, English essayist Joseph Addison asked: "Why may not a whole estate be thrown into a kind of garden?" Washington and Jefferson met this challenge because they combined educated taste with a farmer's knowledge of the land. Having brought a new country into being and set it on its course, both men retired to their farms. The appropriateness of Mount Vernon and the individuality of Monticello reveal their creators' stewardship and unpretentious democratic ideals.

MONTICELLO, Charlottesville, Virginia. The path on the west lawn of Thomas Jefferson's home winds among beds and borders filled with spider flowers, zinnias, and other annuals.

MOUNT VERNON. The entrance drive (above), one of Washington's most original designs, curves through groves on either side of the great lawn. Washington flanked the entry gates with mounds and ha-ha walls, hidden barriers that keep cattle from the bowling green without interrupting the view from the house. Washington organized his kitchen garden (facing) into decorative patterns. Espaliered fruit trees line the south- and west-facing walls, and cordoned apple trees run the length of the garden on either side of the central path.

MOUNT VERNON. *French honeysuckle
(above), a variety that blooms all summer,
climbs the colonnades at the front of the house.
These covered ways give protected access to the
attached kitchen and gardener's cottage in bad
weather. Prince's feather rises bright red above
the carefully tended herbaceous plants of the
flower garden (facing), a part of Washington's
pleasure grounds probably managed by his
wife, Martha.*

MONTICELLO. The serpentine walk (facing) passes by a European larch, one of the few trees from Jefferson's time still standing, and a fish pond designed to keep catches fresh for several days. Nicotiana (above) blooms in the garden path's border. Jefferson laid out the long beds in 1808 when he decided that "the limited number of our flower beds will too much restrain the variety of flowers in which we might wish to indulge."

MONTICELLO. *Jefferson's mountaintop affords views in every direction. He built the brick pavilion (facing) to give him a place to sit and oversee the progress of his vegetable garden. Excavations of the site and Jefferson's detailed notes guided its reconstruction in 1984. Nearby, maple trees (above) frame the eastern prospect.*

MONTICELLO. Jefferson kept meticulous records of his plants, like the sweet basil in bloom (above), and seems to have grown every vegetable available in his day in Monticello's 1,000-foot-long garden (facing). Jefferson also planted a vineyard and orchard on the property, and planned to stock a woodland animal park with pheasants, peacocks, an elk, and a buffalo.

PACA HOUSE, Annapolis, Maryland. The Chinese Chippendale-style bridge (facing) at the bottom of the garden has been reconstructed as it appears in the background of Charles Willson Peale's late 18th-century portrait of William Paca. A classic example of the colonial pleasure ground, Paca's garden was buried for 60 years under a hotel and a bus station. Aided by Peale's painting and archeological findings, restoration began in 1971. Remains of woody roots gave restorers clues to the identity of original trees and shrubs, including the ornamental boxwoods (above) in one of the four garden "rooms."

PACA HOUSE. Eighteenth-century rose varieties (above) stand out against the green of cedar, wax myrtle, and boxwood hedges in the rose parterre. An aerial view (facing) displays the garden's urban setting. Limited to two city lots, the garden ingeniously superimposes formal parterres on terraces that mimic a riverfront falls estate and lead down to an informal, "wilderness" area. Paca, a lawyer, statesman, and signer of the Declaration of Independence, often used his garden for entertaining out of doors.

ENCLOSED GARDENS

Today, the walled garden answers several needs modern Americans share with their colonial forebears: the instinct for enclosure in a sometimes dangerous world, the desire in urban areas to make the best of a few square feet of land, and the impulse to create an intimate, private space. Working with enclosed gardens, landscape architects draw on regional traditions as varied as the Spanish-inspired courtyards of the Southwest and the formal town house gardens of such southern cities as New Orleans and Charleston.

The Spanish pioneers of the Southwest built their farmsteads and missions in Mediterranean patterns dating back to the Roman Empire. External walls with few or no windows divided the dwelling's interior from the outside world, and a heavy wooden door guarded the single entrance. Within lay a courtyard surrounded by rooms and colonnades. Wherever it appeared, the pattern offered two benefits: the walls gave a measure of protection from thieves, bandits, and other hazards of life in a colonial outpost, and shady corners provided relief in a hot, dry climate.

The adobe-walled courtyard of the Spanish-American colonial dwelling was not a pleasure ground, but a workplace where visitors were as likely to meet a horse or a chicken as the owner of the house. In European gardens of the time, a sculpted central fountain anchored the courtyard's decorative elements. In New Spain, a simple wellhead stood at the courtyard's center, the source of water for laundry, drinking, cooking, and bathing. Underfoot there was hard-packed earth, well-suited to the constant traffic of daily domestic business and easily maintained by sweeping or raking.

To provide shade for this workplace, early settlers planted trees, usually palms and live oaks, in informal groupings. Gradually, as southwestern colonial life became safer, graceful touches softened the style; gates became decorative rather than defensive, and more apertures appeared in the walls. In some Franciscan missions, the monks laid out orchards of peach, pear, olive, and fig trees in their courtyards. In the early 19th century, some California

MISSION CARMEL, Carmel, California. The earliest mission courtyards would have been sparsely planted, but in the 19th century, exotics imported from Africa and South America made the practical workspace a place of beauty. In Mission Carmel's main courtyard (facing), smooth river stones buttress the flower beds, conserving moisture in the dry climate. Magenta bougainvillea and orange lantana (above) form a welcoming arch over the entry to the walled garden.

HERMANN-GRIMA HOUSE, New Orleans, Louisiana. Two old magnolias shade this recently restored garden, and high brick walls provide quiet and privacy just steps away from busy city streets. Filled with lilies, violets, shrimp plants, and herbs, the long privet-bordered flower beds complement the house's narrow verandas.

missions developed striking gardens of native and exotic flowers placed in simple beds or arranged in pots around the courtyard. The mission buildings fell into a period of gradual decay following the Mexican War, but their courtyards and gardens exerted an immediate and permanent influence on architectural and landscape design in the Far West.

The enclosed gardens of New Orleans and Charleston, the two leading seaports of the antebellum South, have also had a lasting effect on regional design. Both cities were founded on peninsulas where land for building was scarce; gardens came to be tightly contained between walls and other houses. In New Orleans's oldest district, the French Quarter, the garden evolved behind the house, out of sight of the street. To keep the rear verandas cool, shade trees, especially oaks and magnolias, dominated the courtyard. The other plantings, laid out in intriguing formal patterns, were designed to be viewed from the verandas and the upper rooms of the house.

Faced with a climate almost as oppressive as New Orleans's, Charlestonians also treated their gardens as a source of shade and coolness. But the Charleston custom of aligning a house's narrow side, not its long front, to the street left room for a garden between one house and the next. This "single-house" plan led to unusually inviting and versatile garden designs.

Typically, a low wall or fence with a gate separated the garden from the street without entirely concealing it. The household glimpsed the life of the street; passersby glimpsed inhabitants, coming and going in the garden or on the two- or three-tiered porch that shaded the house's garden front. The visual interaction between street, garden, and veranda made for a unique combination of seclusion and neighborly openness.

Charlestonians were as likely to stroll or sit in their gardens as gaze down upon them, and they planted interesting flower beds and mixed medium-sized flowering ornamentals between the essential large shade trees. Crape myrtle, redbud, and loquat were favored. Vines clambered on walls and columns, enhancing the connectedness of house and garden.

Even though the Charleston garden was walled and restricted to a small city lot, its design opened the enclosure to social interaction. Its hospitable ambience and mixture of formal and informal plantings offered a charming microcosm of the antebellum estate.

(Facing) BEAUREGARD-KEYES HOUSE, New Orleans, Louisiana. Geometrically patterned beds in the urban garden were designed to be viewed from the balconies of the house. The magnolia is original, and boxwood, wisteria, orange trees, roses, and jasmine are recently planted examples of plants common to mid-19th-century New Orleans gardens.

(Upper right) HEYWARD-WASHINGTON HOUSE, Charleston, South Carolina. Carefully restored using original plots, this garden features the plants that would have been blooming during George Washington's visit to the house in 1791.

(Lower right) Garden Wall, Charleston, South Carolina. An unrestored wall in Charleston gives away the secret of its trompe l'oeil effect, as thin sheets of plaster, scored to look like stone, peel away from brick. A Lady Banks's rose drapes over the wall, and an iron gate lets passersby enjoy the flowering spectacle inside the garden.

57

(Upper and lower left) MISSION SANTA BARBARA, Santa Barbara, California. Almost all of California's mission courtyards have been reconstructed, after falling into extreme disrepair between American annexation in 1848 and the beginnings of restoration in the 1920s. Mission Santa Barbara has a fine colonnade from which to view the garden dominated by huge palm trees.

(Facing) MISSION CARMEL. A stone fountain surrounded by an octagonal pool is characteristic of courtyard gardens in colonial California. The stone aggregate makes a fine texture for walking, and the simple daisies and irises suit this intimate setting.

ANTEBELLUM PLANTATIONS

On the historic plantations of the Deep South, long alleys of live oaks lead to white-columned Greek Revival mansions surrounded by azaleas, camellias, gardenias, dogwoods, redbuds, and crape myrtles. Monuments to the privileged lives of antebellum planters, these showplaces also recall the beginnings of naturalized landscaping in America.

Before the 19th century, most southern colonial gardens imitated the symmetry of 17th-century English and French formal designs—a genre which South Carolina's Middleton Place brilliantly preserves. Gradually, planters began to adopt the principles of natural school landscape designers such as William Kent and Capability Brown, who had revolutionized garden design in 18th-century Britain. Discarding the architectural right angles, mathematical curves, and level planes of the French style, Kent, Brown, and their followers enhanced nature's irregular outlines with manicured but loosely shaped meadows, groves, and shrubberies.

Visitors to Middleton Place can easily contrast colonial and antebellum landscape styles by traveling a few miles down the road to its neighbor, Magnolia Gardens. Like Middleton Place, the plantation was established in the 1670s, and the first garden, a French-inspired design, was laid out in the early 18th century with straight allées, rectangular pools, and formal parterres. Despite the destruction of the house by fire in 1800, the garden remained intact until after 1836, when the Reverend John Drayton inherited the estate upon the death of his older brother.

Drayton, a collector of exotic plants, had traveled widely in Europe and visited country homes in England where natural landscaping prevailed. Soon after his return, he began to enlarge and transform the 10-acre garden. He first reclaimed a large swamp near the house, adding fill, shaping waterways, and planting trees and shrubs. Leaving only two straight walks from the house to the river, he removed the formal hedges, beds, terraces, and greenswards, naturalized formal pools with curving banks, and laid out winding paths. Rather than organizing his flowering shrubs in formal beds, Drayton placed them in clumps

MAGNOLIA PLANTATION, Charleston, South Carolina. In 1840, a doctor ordered Reverend John Grimke Drayton to take up gardening for his health. Redesigning the formal gardens he inherited, Drayton planted azaleas throughout the estate. Like other Low Country planters, he found that the area's rich soil and subtropical climate made his property ideal for 19th-century garden styles that emphasized naturalized plantings.

MAGNOLIA PLANTATION. Magnolias are the preeminent ornamental trees in southern plantation gardens. One of four magnolia species discovered by early plant explorers, the Magnolia grandiflora *was named by Linnaeus in honor of Pierre Magnol, director of the botanic garden at Montpellier, France.*

(Facing) AFTON VILLA, St. Francisville, Louisiana. Spanish moss adds an eerie romance to the gardens of the Deep South. A member of the pineapple family, the plant is an epiphyte, not a parasite, and needs the branches of the oak only for support.

around the lawn and under his shade and ornamental trees, which he grew freely, in the American style, without trimming and shaping.

Azaleas dominated the shrubbery. Throughout his long life, Drayton introduced and cultivated exotic and hybrid species, including the first Indian azaleas imported to America. The increasing availability of brilliant new varieties rapidly made azaleas the flowering plant of choice across the South, and landowners restructured their gardens to accommodate azalea displays. At Middleton Place, an early 20th-century owner planted 30,000 azaleas on the opposite side of the house from the 18th-century gardens.

During the Civil War, Union troops destroyed Drayton's Georgian mansion, which had replaced the estate's first house, but left his garden unharmed. Afterwards, in dire financial straits, he sold most of his 1800-acre plantation, moved a small gothic cottage onto the house site, and opened the garden, now covering 50 acres, to the public. These drastic measures paid off. By the time of his death in 1891, Drayton's collection of azaleas and camellias was attracting visitors from all over the world. In the popular imagination, his flower-filled garden represented the classic antebellum landscape.

The influence of naturalism spread as far west as the great cotton plantations of the Mississippi Delta. Today, Delta estates like Oak Alley and Afton Villa show how the planters cultivated a few striking native elements—live oaks, magnolias, and azaleas—to create an atmosphere of luxury and repose. At Afton Villa, a mile-long curving allée lined with azaleas and live oaks leads to the mansion. Even at Rosedown, a Louisiana plantation garden patterned after formal French models, Martha Turnbull softened the effect of parterres and classical statuary with informal beds of flowers and winding paths which foreshadow the gardenesque principles of Andrew Jackson Downing.

In spring, when the azaleas on these plantations bloom, the contrast between gorgeous flowers and somber trees makes a wild and lovely impression on visitors, meeting the highest aim of the natural landscape school: a strong emotional and sensual appeal. Few places achieve this effect more fully than America's antebellum gardens.

OAK ALLEY, Vacherie, Louisiana. Live oak branches along this formal entrance allée twist into shapes that contrast with the rigid lines of the neoclassical plantation house.

ROSEDOWN PLANTATION, St. Francisville, Louisiana. The latticework gazebo and flower garden radiating from it reflect owner Martha Turnbull's imitation of design elements she had seen at Versailles in 1835. Turnbull artfully mixed formal and informal styles, and Rosedown today features imposing trees and shrubs she planted, including the live oak, crape myrtle, and Japanese evergreens overspreading the azalea-filled parterre.

(Facing) AFTON VILLA. A unique live oak allée that curves with the contours of the land, the mile-long approach avenue at Afton Villa also features a glorious variety of azaleas.

(Above) ROSEDOWN. Martha Turnbull chose much of the sculpture in her garden during a trip to Florence in 1851. After a life of comfort on one of Louisiana's most productive plantations, Turnbull faced hard times at the end of the Civil War. With her son and husband dead, she ran the farm and kept her garden clear by bartering with former slaves.

(Pages 70 and 71) MAGNOLIA PLANTATION. At the most well-kept plantation gardens, the mixture of lowland rivers and swamps, ancient trees, and naturalized woodland plantings of dogwoods, azaleas, and jonquils produces the effect of a primeval forest only slightly enhanced by a gardener's hand.

GARDENESQUE DESIGN

Andrew Jackson Downing was only 26 in 1841 when he published *A Treatise on the Theory and Practice of Landscape Gardening*, a book that revolutionized American garden design. Running quickly through six editions, his work appealed to a growing class of householders and influenced a generation of designers, including Frederick Law Olmsted, who created some of America's great urban parks. Downing himself coordinated early designs for the grounds of the Capitol, White House, and Smithsonian Institution, and would have had a larger effect on the appearance of parks in Washington and other major cities had he not died in 1852 in a steamboat accident.

Downing revered the highlands of the Hudson River around Newburgh, New York, where he grew up. The scenery of the Catskills became the ideal against which he measured all landscapes, and he attempted to recapture some of this beauty in his designs for even the smallest suburban properties.

Determined to influence architecture as well as landscape, Downing challenged the Greek Revival conventions which held sway in the 1830s and 1840s. A Greek Revival house with its white paint and black shutters stood out from its surroundings—usually a greensward shaded by a few stately elms or oaks. Downing thought this highly unnatural. He proposed that houses and their outbuildings should be built of stone, which harmonized better with the land than wood. If a house was built of wood, it needed to be painted in earth colors. He even published palettes of acceptable paints.

In his *Treatise*, Downing illustrated how houses and outbuildings should be placed within fully planned domestic landscapes. He revaled what was aesthetically acceptable, admonished the unsuitable, and presented principles for laying out properties of any size with "taste" and "elegance."

Downing's work interpreted and transformed for his American audience the theories of British gardenesque designers Humphrey Repton and J. C. Loudon. Gardenesque, an outgrowth of the 18th-century natural landscape school, exaggerated natural lushness

(Facing) ROCKWOOD, Brandywine Hundred, Delaware. Joseph Shipley's 211-acre estate fulfills every aspiration of gardenesque design. Closely surrounded by mature plantings, the house's craggy architecture blends in seamlessly with the landscape.

(Above) GEORGE READ HOUSE, New Castle, Delaware. Gardenesque design called for hiding or softening all borders on the property. Here, Boston ivy entwines with English ivy on a fence.

ROCKWOOD. *Improved greenhouse technology allowed Victorians to grow an unprecedented variety of rare and unusual flowers, such as this porcelainlike phalaenopsis orchid (above) in the conservatory. Built in 1857 in the Gothic Revival style, Rockwood represents the rustic look architect and landscape designer Andrew Jackson Downing thought all American houses should have. The intricate leaves and branches of a monkey-puzzle tree, Japanese maple, and magnolia (facing) complement the house's color scheme and architectural detail.*

for emotional effects. Downing noted that formal, symmetrical designs had their place in some gardens, but proposed that tasteful landowners should prefer naturalized plantings that produced the picturesque rather than the merely beautiful.

Downing popularized naturalistic principles that already had been implemented on some large estates in America. Washington and Jefferson had planted natural groves and embellished their farms, but they always tempered aesthetics with utility. As at Mount Vernon and Monticello, gardenesque designs replaced the customary straight driveway to a farm or rural house with a curving line, Hogarth's "line of beauty." Gardenesque design, however, called for curved lines everywhere; paths meandered up, down, and around, encouraging visitors to move at a leisurely pace and admire the subtle beauties of the garden.

Gardenesque theory suggested that beauty be sought through contrast. Open meadows and sunny hillsides were set in sharp juxtaposition to dark vales and dense, tree-shaded allées. To heighten contrast, each element of a garden needed to make the strongest possible impression. Hence, exotic trees or shrubs were much superior to native varieties, unless the native were "ancient." Things were always expected to appear a little more mysterious than they actually were.

Evergreens like hemlocks, pines, larches, and cedars were the usual agents of mystery; these shaggy, melancholic native trees exhibited enough character to compete with exotics. Grouped in small groves or arranged in artful perimeter plantings, they emphasized the unity of a garden and set it apart from neighboring properties.

As a cheerful contrast to the dark evergreen boughs, simple beds of brightly colored flowers and flowering shrubs were scattered around meadowlike lawns. Rustic benches, gazebos, sundials, and at Downing's own estate, rough woven baskets, rounded out the gardenesque landscape and gave gardens a welcoming, lived-in feeling.

The American middle and upper middle classes read Downing's books and applied his theories to their houses and gardens until the end of the 19th century. As the nation became increasingly urban and industrial, his artificial rustic landscapes enabled homeowners to feel a link with vanishing rural traditions. Downing's work strongly reinforced the American ideal of the single family dwelling set within its own garden, an ideal that eventually led to the creation of our vast suburban neighborhoods.

ROCKWOOD. *The gentle curves of rhododendrons in bloom harmonize with shaggy conifers and natural granite outcroppings. Nineteenth-century American gardeners did not restrict plants to borders, beds, and parterres, but let them punctuate the lawn. While the ''Japanese'' garden, complete with rocks, streams, and wooden temples, was soon to attract the eye of many Victorian gardeners, Rockwood's solemn naturalism is actually much closer to Oriental gardening principles. Recently restored, Rockwood's flamboyant conservatory (facing) contains palms, ferns, banana trees, and a wealth of other exotics.*

GEORGE READ HOUSE. Designed in 1847-48, the Read garden illustrates the mixed group of aesthetic ideals current at the time. A formal boxwood parterre, an ornamental fence, and a Downingesque wooded park surround the earlier Federal-style house. Downing preferred naturalistic plantings to formal beds, because, as he wrote, "the manifestation of power is to many minds far more captivating than that of beauty."

VICTORIAN FLOWER GARDENS

Americans have always made a place for colorful and interesting flowers in their gardens. Pilgrim housewives brought seeds for pansies as well as cabbages to the colonies. Washington and Jefferson rejected English naturalist Capability Brown's recommendation that lawns and groves completely replace the flower garden. But domestic gardens were dominated by the color green until the middle of the 19th century, when advances in science and changes in taste produced an explosion of colorful floral decoration.

English and American botanists had been importing subtropical plants since the 17th century, but only a very small percentage of those shipped survived the long voyages. Then, in the 1830s, plant explorers began using the terrarium, a glass container with an airtight seal that kept plants alive in transport. Seeds, bulbs, and cuttings of impatiens, petunias, dahlias, peonies, and many other gloriously colored flowers from Central and South America, Africa, and the Orient began pouring into European and American greenhouses. In England, the end of the luxury tax on glass spurred commercial gardeners to build much larger, brighter greenhouses. Now they and their American counterparts had room to cultivate and propagate these imports and to experiment with hybridizing older varieties of flowering plants.

Changes in the American household brought about by the industrial revolution also played a part in the genesis of the Victorian flower garden. With prosperity for the upper classes and an expanding immigrant labor force, a substantial number of women could afford servants. Victorian society, however, offered Victorian "ladies" few opportunities for work outside the home. Limited to the domestic arena, but freed from household chores, women became increasingly concerned with matters of color, design, taste, and culture. Horticulture, landscape design, and flower gardening offered accepted avenues for personal expression.

Victorian women were not content to leave their age's bounty of flowers outdoors. Nineteenth-century interiors displayed an unprecedented wealth of floral motifs covering tapestries, mirrors, carpets, woodwork, and plasterwork. Victorian women produced

CELIA THAXTER'S GARDEN, Appledore Island, Maine. A poet and hostess to artists and writers of the day, Thaxter became as well known for her garden as she was for her hospitality. The flowers in the 50-by-15-foot fenced plot have been restored to follow the plan in her 1894 autobiography, An Island Garden. *Shirley and Oriental poppies, coreopsis, cornflowers, and marigolds grow profusely in the eastern beds.*

drawings and paintings of flowers and hung them on walls. They embellished trays and table tops with pressed flower collages mounted under glass. Potted plants crowded parlors and conservatories. Exotics like palms and monkey-puzzle trees, bird-of-paradise flowers and calla lilies were combined with ingenious planters and vases to form dramatic displays. A publication of the time pictures a dining table with two holes near the center through which potted palms rise up and overspread dinner guests with their fronds.

Indoors and out, the dominant color was red: red rooms, covered in scarlet wallpaper, and red flower beds, filled with hybrid geraniums and nasturtiums. Whatever flowers they featured, these beds were usually islands cut into the lawn near the house, extending the creative excess of the interior; sheer profusion made home and garden visually coherent.

Two major types of Victorian flower gardens were popular in America, and they may be said to express the double nature of the Victorian personality. Most gardeners plunged forward with the tide of scientific and industrial progress, creating intricate, massed banks of hybrids and exotics, a practice known as bedding-out. The flowers most frequently associated with bedding-out included geraniums, ageratum, salvia, alyssum, petunias, verbena, and heliotrope. Red cannas were by far the most popular flowers in subtropical beds; tall purple-leaved varieties were often used at the back or center, with dwarf hybrids set around the edges. Broad-leaved crotons, bananas, caladiums, or palms, with wandering jew as a ground cover, also made a startling display.

The results were often more public than private. One estate owner in New Jersey planted over a million plants in four beds so tightly packed with flowers that they looked like huge Oriental carpets spread out on the grass. Others created plantings that looked like clocks, flags, ribbons, and other fanciful figures.

Some Victorians, however, looked back to earlier times when life seemed calmer and safer. Their nostalgic cottage gardens were composed almost entirely of old-fashioned flowers: monkshood, love-lies-bleeding, hollyhocks, angelicas, marigolds, foxgloves, primroses, violets, and antique roses. These beds intermingled plants of different heights, colors, shapes, scents, and textures in compositions that based their attraction not on overwhelming numbers or flamboyant patterns, but on the beauty and form of the flower itself.

CELIA THAXTER'S GARDEN. Thaxter placed her garden on the sunny terrace between her cottage and the sea. Although most of the flowers have had to be painstakingly researched and restored, the day lilies by the gate may have been planted by Thaxter nearly 100 years ago.

BRUCEMORE. Brucemore's owners tried many of the hybrid delphiniums that became available in the 19th century, while Celia Thaxter's garden featured some of the sparsely blossomed annual varieties, like those Bartram and Jefferson grew.

(Facing) CELIA THAXTER'S GARDEN. In summer, a constellation of yellow coreopsis stands out against the green tangle of honeysuckle and wisteria vines on the north fence. Thaxter's parents were the lighthouse keepers on White Island when Celia was a child. Her love of modest plants was born in those lonely years; she later wrote that ''every blade of grass that sprang out of the ground, every humblest weed was precious in my sight.''

BRUCEMORE. Caroline Sinclair built the Queen Anne-style home (left) in 1886 and planted a garden of annuals and perennials, focusing on snapdragons and roses. The second owner, Irene Douglas, expanded the beds, possibly basing her designs on the work of turn-of-the-century English designer Gertrude Jekyll. Jekyll, who combined the eye of an impressionist painter with the knowledge of a horticulturalist, was an important force in late Victorian garden design. While the cast-iron deer (facing) has long been a denizen of Brucemore's garden, the ornamental fence replaced a wire and wooden post fence in the middle of this century.

ECLECTIC GARDENS

At the end of the 19th century, very little garden design was specifically American. Landowners admired the complex and exotic designs of gardens in foreign cultures and decided they could try them all. Italian gardens jostled Japanese gardens, divided only by small Greek temples or elaborate French rose parterres. Alongside these foreign gardens, what little had been salvaged from early American horticulture and design was packaged as the American colonial garden, usually represented by herbs planted in intricate patterns.

Eclectic garden design was itself borrowed from Britain, whose far-flung empire had brought decorative and horticultural ideas home to the mother country. If an 18th-century room could be made over to resemble the interior of a Turkish tent, there was no reason why a Japanese tea garden should seem at all peculiar behind a Victorian Gothic house. The eclectic garden compartmented and exhibited each style as if it were an illustration in one of the home and garden improvement books of the day.

Eclecticism flourished on large estates and in small gardens alike. Italian gardens were the most common, constructed with hedges, clipped trees and shrubs, and thousands of flowers bedded-out into decorative patterns. The flower beds were not authentically Italian, but eclectic gardeners never insisted that every detail ring true. Next in popularity, the Oriental garden, most often "Japanese," showed an even freer hand; Victorians were deeply curious about Eastern culture, but were largely ignorant of Oriental garden theories.

Many estates added horticultural theme gardens and other specialty gardens to their mix of cultural styles. Depending upon local growing conditions, gardeners designed cactus gardens, fern gardens, rose gardens, and pansy gardens. Scented gardens featured plants chosen solely for their fragrances. The rock garden appeared in a variety of forms, from sculptural gardens that piled stones under and around statues to hillside gardens that placed rugged buildings amid alpine flowers and evergreens. Color gardens taxed the ingenuity of

(Facing) SONNENBERG, Canandaigua, New York. In 1901, Mary Clark Thompson began filling every corner of her 50-acre estate with theme gardens. Restoration efforts underway since 1972 have brought to life the long-neglected wonders of the rose garden, which contains thousands of bushes extended like an amphitheater around a classical belvedere.

(Above) MORRIS ARBORETUM, Chestnut Hill, Pennsylvania. Victorians had a passion for ferns, even displaying them in glass cases in their parlors. For their diverse collection, John Morris and his sister Lydia built what is now the country's only extant 19th-century fernery.

gardeners, who composed these decorative plantings with blooms of only one or two colors. Most inventive, perhaps, were the moonlight gardens, which combined white blossoms with white marble to provide a place for romantic nighttime strolls.

Eclectic design, with its dependence on an abundance of diverse new plant material, followed the mid-century flood of hybrids and imported plants. Innovations in greenhouse construction made possible the propagation of these plants, particularly annual flowers. Improved heating systems gave more exact temperature control, and cast iron provided support for larger panes of glass, allowing commercial growers to build greenhouses big enough for their expanding mail-order seed businesses.

Most greenhouses were strictly functional, providing winter protection for tender species, as they had done since Washington's time, but Victorians also constructed decorative greenhouses ornamented with imaginative ironwork. Some greenhouses were designed to keep plants like palms and tree ferns inside throughout the year, and some were constructed as indoor vineyards.

The conservatory, another variation on the greenhouse, combined profuse plant displays with inventive architecture. Attached to the house so that plants could be seen and cared for daily, the conservatory usually opened to the living room or parlor through glass French doors. It was fashionable for women to serve tea in the conservatory, where they could entertain their friends in an exotic environment without having to leave the house.

The most interesting eclectic gardens, like Sonnenberg in Canandaigua, New York, and the Morris Arboretum in Chestnut Hill, Pennsylvania, were designed and directed by one or two creative individuals, gardeners who mixed styles while avoiding the ponderous tone of an exhibition. Another such garden is Green Animals, a combination topiary and Colonial Revival garden in Portsmouth, Rhode Island, begun by Thomas Brayton in 1880. His daughter Alice, who saw to its care and expansion until her death in 1972, once said that she thought gardens should be cheerful places, filled with liveliness and lightness. Her family's success in achieving this quality sets Green

MORRIS ARBORETUM. The Morrises fed swans from the Love Temple in the days when Morris Arboretum was their private estate.

Animals apart from many Victorian eclectic gardens.

This exceptionally well-maintained garden contains more than 50 examples of topiary, a 2,000-year-old art that became immensely popular in Victorian times. At Green Animals, a horse and rider, donkey, elephant, mountain goat, ostrich, and menagerie of other beasts, all fashioned from privet, stand guard over precisely trimmed boxwood borders, fruit trees, and bright formal flower beds. Although topiary has been called a "naive" form of garden art, the process of taming privet and boxwood with wires, trimming buds and branches, and repairing storm and drought damage calls for intensive and intricate labor.

The Brayton house's plain Victorian architecture matches the modest effects of its garden. Much of the landscaping has a colonial flavor: the house sits on a hill overlooking the water, a broad lawn stretches out in front, and a few tulip poplars tower over the side yard. Behind are the outbuildings, the Colonial Revival garden dominated by the topiary, and an extensive herb garden. Narrow gravel paths run in strict configurations around the boxwood beds.

Like a colonial garden, Green Animals contains many fruits, primarily peaches in several varieties, grown within the boxwood hedges and underplanted with bulbs in spring and gaily colored annuals in summer. Through the 19th century, peaches were a major agricultural crop in Rhode Island; orchards near Narragansett Bay supplied the cities of Boston, Providence, and New York with abundant fruit during the summer months.

MORRIS ARBORETUM. Sycamores and maples brighten the naturalized woodland of the Arboretum. Begun in 1887, the grounds include an Italian rose garden, Japanese garden, Spanish garden, rustic garden with a log cabin, and an English pastoral landscape complete with cattle.

Other fruits in the garden include old-fashioned varieties of blueberries, gooseberries, and raspberries. In summer, figs in full leaf add a Mediterranean exoticism to the composition. An arbor covered with gourds, which becomes a little orange outdoor room in autumn, completes this spirited garden.

Thomas Brayton's whimsical vision and his daughter Alice's devoted care assured the endurance of their eclectic garden through several periods of changing taste in garden design. Carefully maintained today by the Preservation Society of Newport County, Green Animals offers modern visitors a window into the Victorian age.

SONNENBERG. Constructed by artist K. Wadamori and six Japanese workmen over a period of six months, Sonnenberg's Japanese Garden (above) was designed according to Oriental principles. It features a wooden bridge, a bronze statue of Buddha, a restored teahouse, meticulous rockwork, and a diverse mix of conifers, including Japanese red pine and umbrella pine. Twenty-five thousand flowers form the fleur-de-lis and scimitar patterns in the Italian Garden (facing); the plants bedded-out here include coleus and dusty miller.

SONNENBERG. Color gardens were a charming eccentricity of the Victorian age. Owner Mary Thompson called her blue and white garden (facing and lower right) the Intimate Garden, and it was her favorite on the estate. The flowers include peonies, phlox, snapdragons, vinca, delphiniums, anchusia, salvia, and irises. She chose white marble for all the structural elements. Sonnenberg's rock garden (upper right) was designed to have as many mini-environments as possible so that a variety of plants could thrive. Unlike most rock gardens, it incorporates streams, waterfalls, simulated springs hidden in grottos, pools fed by geysers, and a stone-columned overlook.

95

GREEN ANIMALS, Portsmouth, Rhode Island. Thomas and Alice Brayton's Colonial Revival garden fills seven-and-a-half acres with roses, herbs, grapevines, berries, and fruit trees. The topiary animals are the garden's pride. Shaped from privet, they tower above its maze and seasonal flower beds. Strong enough to withstand salt air and storm damage, privet can be repaired by planting new whips and encouraging them to interweave. Green Animals also features topiary arches, an armchair, and a two-masted schooner.

(Pages 98-99) MORRIS ARBORETUM. Even the Arboretum's benches illustrate eclectic tastes. Yellow leaves scattered over the terrace have fallen from a Chinese ginkgo, one of the most primitive and ancient of trees.

MORRIS ARBORETUM. Japanese maples (above), fiery red in autumn, were introduced into American gardens about 1890; the Arboretum is known for its Oriental trees and shrubs. Camperdown elms (facing) have been popular ornamental trees since colonial times. The elm's pendulous branches provide a sheltered garden room in summer and a fantastically gnarled living sculpture in winter.

GREAT ESTATES

Lavish symbols of the Gilded and Jazz Ages, the mansions built in the United States between the 1880s and the 1930s often featured equally opulent gardens. Even though the designers of these great estates were the first Americans to create formal gardens that stretched as far as the eye could see, their landscapes sometimes served only as a kind of foliated theatrical setting for the mansion.

Models for the great estates were predominantly European, although a few "colonial" houses were constructed in this period. Industrial and financial barons, their architects, interior designers, and landscape gardeners favored Renaissance Italian or 17th-century French palace and landscape designs because these periods epitomized wealth and power. Time has lent romance to the gardens of America's great estates, but that was not the owners' original intent. When these "country places" were built, they were bold expressions of a few men's dominance over the land and over other men.

Many rich 19th-century Americans took the grand tour in their youth or lived in Europe for long periods, and it may be said that the great estate was born during these extended holidays. Landowners shipped back thousands of crates filled with European columns, arches, mantels, sculptures, fountains, and wellheads. More important, their designers closely studied the country houses of southern England, the parks and gardens of Paris, and the villas of Florence. With imported materials and firsthand observation, designers could return home to accurately duplicate European styles.

Dumbarton Oaks, in Washington, D.C., is representative of the gardens created in America during this period. The ancient villas of Rome and Renaissance estates of France, Italy, and England influenced the renovation of its architecture and landscape, but Dumbarton escapes the imitative excesses of many great estates to make a coherent design statement all its own. The garden reveals the originality and creative cooperation of Dumbarton's owner, Mildred Barnes Bliss, and its landscape architect, Beatrix Farrand.

(Facing) THE ELMS, Newport, Rhode Island. One of Newport's most interesting seaside "cottages," The Elms closely follows French models, particularly in its use of statuary and intricate flower beds.

VIZCAYA, Key Biscayne, Florida. Whether they placed fanciful frogs on an Italian fountain or classical deities in a French garden, great estate designers and owners brought European sculpture to America in unprecedented numbers.

DUMBARTON OAKS, Washington, D.C. Beatrix Farrand and many other great estate designers often designed furniture especially for their gardens. Her beautifully scalloped teakwood bench faces east over the rose garden.

Bliss lived for many years in France, where she visited the great châteaux near Paris and explored smaller gardens in remote sections of the country. On these expeditions, she gathered ideas and bought garden ornaments with the intention of eventually incorporating them into a garden of her own. Her opportunity came in 1920, when she and her husband returned to America and bought an old farmhouse and land overlooking Rock Creek in Georgetown. Bliss chose Farrand to bring the restful ambience of a French country garden to her new estate. Farrand, an Anglophile, a niece of Edith Wharton, and the only woman among the 11 founding members of the American Society of Landscape Architects, found the greatest inspirations of her career in the property and in Bliss's enthusiasm.

Bliss asked her to create essentially formal gardens that would provide year-round interest. To achieve this effect, Farrand designed strongly articulated areas like the terrace gardens and planted coniferous and broad-leaved evergreens. Many sections of the garden are entirely green, with ground covers chosen for contrasting leaf forms and textures. Deciduous trees and ornamental shrubs provide color, but they enhance rather than dominate the structural scheme.

Lawrence White, son of renowned architect Stanford White, renovated the house. His music room, loggia, and swimming pool express an atmosphere of elegant ease. White added many southern European architectural details, including the arches of the loggia, stuccoed surface of the building walls, and tiled floor and roof of the orangery.

Water displays, sculptures, and other ornaments, including antique clay pots gathered by Bliss on the Riviera, add to the Mediterranean atmosphere. Farrand arranged graceful columns and urns behind the little amphitheater on the far eastern edge of the garden. She had seen similar features at the garden of Raxa, where urns flank a staircase leading high up into the Majorcan hills. Two statues of smiling cherubs holding dolphins make the fountain terrace seem authentically French. Foxglove, columbine, sweet william, borage, campanula, and coral bells bordering the lawn have the same old-world charm as those in country gardens near Fontainebleau.

In the wisteria arbor, one of the garden's most delightful places, the flowers' fragrance combines with shade and the sound of water splashing from a French lead fountainhead. Large clay pots of lemon trees, loquats, oleanders, lantanas, and olives, interspersed with smaller pots of geraniums and sweet-scented herbs, including balm, lavender hyssop, catmint, rue, and wormwood supplement the wisteria's heavy scent.

Bliss and Farrand wanted to make their garden look as established as the European gardens that inspired it; ornaments and walls were roughened and plantings were naturalized to appear as if they were "found" on the site. Many great estate owners and designers tried to endow their gardens with the refinement and authority of the historic homes they admired. With the help of time, Dumbarton Oaks is one of the few that has achieved this character.

In this period of pervasive foreign influence, a handful of estate designers espoused the principle that culture and climate alone should determine how a garden looks. One such designer, a revolutionary in an age of imitation, was Jens Jensen, who came to the United States from Denmark in 1884. It is an interesting comment on the age of the great estates that an immigrant, inspired by the plains and forests of the Midwest, designed the most fully American gardens.

Insisting that native plants and landscapes, not European artifacts and spatial concepts, must be the essence of American garden design, Jensen composed his prairie-style designs with vast numbers of indigenous trees and shrubs. To find these plants he sent workmen and suppliers to the wilderness and backwoods; American nurseries, thriving on the demand for exotics, kept meager stocks of native plants. In Jensen's most notable gardens, established at several Ford family estates in Michigan, elms, oaks, maples, redbuds, and hawthorns stand in generous, loosely curving groves, separated by broad, grassy expanses that evoke America's wide skies and open spaces.

EDSEL AND ELEANOR FORD ESTATE, Grosse Pointe Shores, Michigan. The broad lawn extending from the house to Lake St. Clair is typical of the work of Jens Jensen, the Danish-born founder of the prairie style in American landscape design. Jensen found inspiration in the play of the sky and sun over the prairies' open spaces.

BILTMORE HOUSE, Asheville, North Carolina. Frederick Law Olmsted, designer of New York's Central Park, adapted his naturalistic style to suit George Washington Vanderbilt's 250-room château. In a landscape design that influenced many subsequent great estates, he created formal gardens and a long lawn stretching from the house to a statue of Diana (facing). But the entrance drive is pure gardenesque, winding for three miles in and out of woods and offering no glimpse of the house until the very end. Olmsted took on the immense project of designing Biltmore's grounds from 1889 to 1896 mainly so that he could plant an American arboretum to rival Kew Gardens in London. His grove (right) was just a beginning. Vanderbilt's financial difficulties prevented the completion of the arboretum. Later, however, the nation's first forestry school was established on the grounds, which then comprised 125,000 acres of hardwoods and pines.

BILTMORE HOUSE. Olmsted's hedge and shrub garden (facing) provides a subtle transition from the terraces of the Italian Garden to the wilder landscape beyond. Throughout the estate, massive plantings of laurels, hollies, boxwoods, and rhododendrons smooth the progression from Biltmore's formal gardens to the surrounding forests. In Biltmore's walled garden (above), one of the world's largest, elaborately bedded salvias and chrysanthemums and an imposing greenhouse create a formal grandeur. The vine-covered pergola marks the design as Olmsted's. He once wrote: "I urge you to hunt for beauty in commonplace and peasant conditions…rustic stables, sheds…pergolas and trellises, seats and resting places…and all such things as are made lovely by growths that seem to be natural and spontaneous to the place, especially vines."

VIZCAYA. The period's most authentic Italian garden was designed by Diego Suarez for industrialist James Deering. Built between 1914 and 1921, the gardens closely follow the Italian model: extensive waterworks, classical statuary, and intricate plantings of trimmed evergreens. Suarez brilliantly adapted the style to the Florida climate by fashioning the skyline with native live oaks rather than European cypresses.

111

VIZCAYA. Leaded glass doors (facing) look past the south patio to an artificial hill terraced with perfectly proportioned water cascades. Suarez built the hill to recreate in Florida's flat terrain the terraces which are characteristic of Italian villas. In Vizcaya's **giardino segreto,** *or secret garden (above), bands of stone rocaille work resemble stalactites. Common in Italian and French estate gardens, rocaille was widely used near water features.*

NAUMKEAG, Stockbridge, Massachusetts. Naumkeag's grounds reflect the cooperation of owner Mabel Choate and landscape architect Fletcher Steele. According to Steele, the view he composed to the west of woods, apple orchard, fields, and the Berkshires (facing) ''was the first attempt to incorporate the form of background topography into foreground details in a unified design.'' The moon gate (above), added in 1955, completed the Chinese Garden.

NAUMKEAG. Naumkeag, an Indian word,
means ''haven of peace,'' but Steele's designs
are often more playful than tranquil. Built in
1938, the Birch Walk zigzags up a steep hill
through paper birches. A stream flows beneath
the staircase and gushes into the niches behind
each of the four landings.

FILOLI, Woodside, California. Filoli's land-scape architect Bruce Porter gained his inspiration from the Pre-Raphaelite movement in English painting. He and florist Isabella Worn gave Filoli's English-style "garden of rooms" a medieval atmosphere by enclosing the estate's gardens with walls, groves, and tall yew hedges. The new display garden (facing), filled with herbs and annuals, replaced the kitchen garden which supplied the estate with vegetables and cutting flowers. Clematis overhangs the entry of mining and winery magnate William Bourn's house (upper right), designed by architect Willis Polk as an amalgam of Flemish, French, Spanish, and English styles. In Filoli's walled garden (lower right), azaleas, camellias, orna-mental fruit trees, and other flowering plants produce a fluid design within an enclosed space.

FILOLI. Porter's designs marvelously balance
formal structure and romantic embellishment:
a camperdown elm and climbing hydrangea
decorate a walk along a brick wall (above). In
the Sunken Garden (facing), a rectangular pool
leads the eye past a blooming sunburst honey
locust and on to the Coast Range.

FILOLI. *The outline of the low boxwood hedges in the Chartres Cathedral Garden (facing) was inspired by one of the famous medieval windows. Filoli has more textural interest than is usually expected from a West Coast garden, where the emphasis is often on structure and flowering plants. The Knot Garden (above), based on medieval herb gardens, intertwines germander and lavender cotton.*

DUMBARTON OAKS. Beatrix Farrand once wrote that gardeners "must notice the different lights and shadows and see how they change the effect; they must remember the plants whose scent begins at dusk and those whose fragrance stops with the light...they must learn to know the sounds of the leaves on different sorts of trees." Dumbarton Oaks beautifully illustrates these design ideals. Rough rocks and benches, surrounded by a riotous tangle of forsythia (above), make a primitive and delightful garden niche. An aerial view (facing) shows how Farrand brilliantly integrated her formal designs with the estate's existing topography and trees. The strong forms of the enclosed gardens and the water features are distributed among large trees, carefully pruned to allow sufficient light to penetrate to the lawns and flower beds.

124

DUMBARTON OAKS. Seasonal flower displays—tulips in
spring, annuals in summer, and chrysanthemums in fall—
contrast with the informal plantings outside the Terrace Garden
wall (facing), including a flowering dogwood framed by an
American holly tree and a European beech. Owner Mildred
Bliss asked Farrand to create the atmosphere of an older garden
reminiscent of the ones she had visited in the French countryside, an effect achieved by sculpture like the urn at the entry to
the pool house (above).

EDSEL FORD ESTATE. Jens Jensen planned the grounds of large estates without regard to the architectural style of the house. He filled his landscapes with native trees, placing hardwoods like these maples and oaks (above and facing) in informal, sheltering groves.

EDSEL FORD ESTATE. Secluded in a grove of dogwoods, redbuds, and hemlocks, the estate's swimming pool (above) contrasts dynamically with Exbury azaleas and birches on the lawn. Jensen sought to emphasize the unique design qualities of each tree species. The thin, brown twigs and dark, ridged trunks of black willows (facing) etch an elaborate pattern on a winter day.

MODERN CALIFORNIA GARDENS

California's weather and history have always given its horticulture and architecture a distinct regional character. The mild climate suits an enormous range of ornamental plants; West Coast gardens have contained specimens from Australia, New Zealand, Mexico, South America, Africa, China, and Japan since the 19th century. The state's strong Spanish colonial heritage made stucco and tile common building materials in mansions as well as bungalows. But before World War II, California landscape design conformed to the same eclectic principles that prevailed throughout the country. Great estates of the 1920s and 1930s, like San Simeon and Filoli, took their inspiration from European models.

After World War II, however, a small group of landscape architects in California revolted against the prevailing dependence on imported forms and created the first important modern gardens in America. Led by Thomas Church and Garrett Eckbo, this school sought to design gardens that suited American landscapes, plants, and social customs. Eckbo succinctly stated the group's rejection of eclectic and great estate gardens in a paraphrase of the French architect Le Corbusier:

> There has never been an English garden outside of England, a Spanish garden outside of Spain, a Japanese garden outside of Japan. There has never been an Italian Renaissance garden since the Italian Renaissance, never an American colonial garden since the vigorous beginning of the American states.

Responding to this challenge, the California school first changed the garden's relationship to the house. Church made gardens outdoor rooms. As some Victorian conservatories and gardenesque cottages had done, Church's designs played with the barrier between indoors and outdoors: long beds of plants, including banana trees, grow close to both sides of a living room's curved, glass wall; a front door opens directly into a garden; a bench extends through the window of a pool pavilion, serving as a seat on both sides of the glass.

California designers defined each garden room with hard edges. Plants were used mainly for accent and softening, and stone paving and concrete covered much of the earth and formed boundaries between each part of the garden. Nothing, in fact, more clearly

PHILLIPS HOUSE, Napa, California. Postwar California landscape architects made concrete and other hard materials as much a part of their designs as flowers and trees. Set in a rectangular island of concrete softened by corner scallops and double coping, Thomas Church's pool design blends with the sky rather than the garden.

distinguished the California garden than its imaginative use of concrete. The California school took advantage of concrete's plasticity; it could be poured into molds of any shape. The surface could be smoothed, brushed, or scored. When subtly colored beach pebbles were added to the mix, the resulting surface glistened in rain or fog. Designers used concrete to mold planters and benches in place and to retain terraces. Fences, no longer utilitarian dividers, became abstract sculptures that dramatically organized garden spaces.

Church formed concrete into broad, sweeping curves, creating immense terraces. Eckbo explored the complicated interactions of mixing, forming, and finishing, and his work emphasized textures and sculptural forms. He worked with sculptors to provide a sympathetic environment for their work, and his use of freestanding screens and beds

was sculptural in itself. Trees with multiple stems or unusual bark or leaves were also treated as sculpture and emphasized with special plantings and night lighting. Church's designs often shaped themselves around large live oaks already on the property.

Although California's climate suits many plant varieties, low rainfall in many parts of the state makes irrigation an important part of gardening. For this reason, Church kept lawns small, and set plantings within range of garden hoses. The California school's planting design was restrained, but brilliantly juxtaposed native and exotic plants. One of the most common contrasts is between the rounded darkness of the California live oak and the silvery grey verticality of the Australian eucalyptus.

THOMAS CHURCH HOUSE, San Francisco, California. In his own back garden, Church shakes up traditional expectations with a whimsical mix of formal and informal elements: boxwoods, roses, and a statue are joined by clay pots, a wooden trellis, and a wisteria vine.

(Facing) DONNELL HOUSE, Sonoma, California. In a characteristic Church design, gaillardia, a plant native to the West, makes a bright progression up a dry hillside.

Such rigorously designed landscapes do not suit every gardener; most Americans let plants determine garden structure, and many continue to adapt English and European designs. Church's and Eckbo's gardens, however, have influenced large and small landscape designs for 40 years, and their ideas, once revolutionary, no longer shock. It is difficult to imagine two more different gardens than the raised herb beds at the Whipple House and the modern terraces at Church's Donnell House, but in creating convenient spaces for outdoor living, the designers of the California school made gardens once again useful places, and bound together a 300-year-old native tradition.

DEFORREST HOUSE, Santa Barbara, California. Elizabeth and Lockwood DeForrest published The Santa Barbara Gardener *from 1925 until 1942 to explain and illustrate the unique conditions of California horticulture. They brought their expertise to bear in their own garden, a set of firmly structured garden rooms that feature densely planted native varieties.*

(Page 138) BROOKE HOUSE, Woodside, California. Inventive use of rocks and paving marks Church's poolside garden. Rhododendrons, Japanese maples, chrysanthemums, and a miniature woodland of other plants take full advantage of the sunny terrace.

(Page 139) HANSEN HOUSE, San Francisco, California. For this small urban courtyard garden, Church fit a symmetrical, old-fashioned design of three-brick squares in an asymmetrical space with a border of irregular flagstones set within a frame.

PHILLIPS HOUSE. Perhaps the most striking feature of this Napa Valley garden is the incredible diversity of trees, including oranges, apples, magnolias, and cypresses, that Church used to blend the clean lines of the contemporary house with the surrounding woods and vineyards.

DONNELL HOUSE. Church had a genius for combining angles and curves. In the Donnell garden (facing), the matching arcs of the hedge, the lawn, and the asphalt walk shape a graceful entrance to the house. The curvilinear expanse of the swimming pool deck (above) is cleverly composed of planks arranged in large parquet-like squares—one of the most influential designs in recent history. Live oaks grow through the deck and become living sculptures.

EDSEL FORD ESTATE. Sugar maple in autumn.

PHOTOGRAPHY CREDITS